Thi

THE
BLACK
DEATH
AND OTHER PUTRID PLAGUES
OF
London

D0526239

First published in 2002 by Watling St Publishing
The Old Chapel
East End
Northleach
Gloucestershire
GL54 3PQ

Printed in Thailand

Copyright © Watling St Publishing Ltd 2002

ISBN 1-904153-01-1

24681097531

Cover design and illustration: Mark Davis
Cartoons: Martin Angel

THE BLACK DEATH
AND OTHER PUTRID PLAGUES OF
London

Natasha Narayan

WATLING STREET

Natasha Narayan has worked as a journalist in Albania, Bosnia, Georgia and the former Soviet Union. She was also briefly education correspondent on the *Observer*, a waitress, a satellite TV presenter and one of those annoying telesales people. She lives in North London with her husband and daughter.

For Paul and Nina with love.

Contents

Introduction

Plague and pestilence were as much a fact of life to our ancestors as zits and homework are to us (however bad our spots are, believe me, they're nothing compared to putrid pestilence).

Our ancestors didn't know what caused poxy plague. They thought of it as a beautiful young maiden who would kidnap them and give them the kiss of death. Or as a horseman who would ride into town on a black charger cutting people down as he went with his shining scythe.

Slash! – there goes another ten children. Slash! – there goes a mum and dad.

When plague attacked London in 1348 it killed one in every three people. Bodies lay in the street and as there weren't enough cemeteries to go round, the dead were thrown into great big pits.

In those days there was no business like the death business. Londoners became so cosy with death they would even arrange family picnics in the graveyard. Yuck, a day out in a cemetery. Sounds creepy, doesn't it?

No one expected to live very long and they certainly didn't expect their kids to stick around. Children were hacked down in

greater numbers by pestilence than their parents were –
because the bugs much preferred fresh young lamb to stringy
old mutton.

Parents ignored their kids and there were often accidents
when they would fall into the fire or the cooking pot. (But at
least medieval Londoners were better than the Romans, who
would simply dump children they didn't want in the forests to be
devoured by wild beasts.) Perhaps our great-great-great-
great[you get the idea]-grandparents were more like animals
who expect some of their huge litter to die than a doting
modern mum and dad.

Even among royal circles – which had the best food and
doctors – children died by the coffin-load. Queen Anne had
seventeen or eighteen children (history hasn't counted them
exactly) but when she died in 1714, not a single one of them was
still alive. Perhaps the poor Queen died of exhaustion.

As if plague and pestilence weren't bad enough our ancestors
also had to cope with war, famine, back-breaking labour, stinky
houses, nasty nobles – the list of their misfortunes goes on and on.
It's a wonder they lived long enough for the plague to get them.

Forty-five isn't very old nowadays (your parents will kid you
that it is, in fact, the prime of life). But Londoners in those times
of pestilence who lived to forty-five would be haggard and

probably have black teeth – if they had any teeth at all, that is.

There are so many nasty illnesses and facts in this book – from the medicine made of snails with powdered peacock dung, to the dustbin man who drowned in a cesspit full of pooh – that by the time you've finished reading it you might be a bit haggard yourself!

Edward & Edward & Edward & Edward & Edward & Edward ... Gibbon

Edward Gibbon, the great historian (author of the very, very long *The Decline and Fall of the Roman Empire*), born in 1773, wrote in his memoirs about how miserable his childhood was as the oldest of six children. 'I was succeeded by five brothers and one sister, all of whom were snatched away in their infancy ... of any given number [of children] born the greater number are extinguished [die] before their ninth year.'

So sure were the young Edward Gibbon's parents that he would die that they called all his brothers Edward too. (It must have been very confusing at mealtimes. 'Edward, pass the brussels sprouts. No, not you, Ed. Not you either, Eddie. That Edward.) It was a sad fact that the oldest Edward, who his parent's thought was a definite gonner, was the only one to live.

CHAPTER ONE

The Black Death

> Ring a ring a rosie
> A pocket full of posies
> A-tishoo ... a-tishoo
> We all fall down
>
> Does rosie stand for A) a rash B) roses C) a medieval
> cinnamon bun?
>
> Answer) a) Rosies were the black-spotted rash that appeared
> on plague victims' bodies. People carried posies of flowers to
> ward off the evil smell of the plague. 'A-tishoo' was the
> sneezing, which was one of the first signs of the plague and
> 'We all fall down' ... Well that's obvious, isn't it?

Think of chickenpox, mumps and measles mixed with flu, fever,
whooping cough and really, really bad acne and you still haven't
got anywhere near the yucky, scary horridness of the dreaded
Black Death.

When you think of a plague you probably imagine a swarm of
microscopic bugs munching up everything that gets in their way.
But in 1348, when the dreaded bubonic plague first sailed into
London from China there weren't any microscopes or scientists
in white lab coats. They didn't know what had hit them. In

England a million people died – about one in every three people. In some poorer areas of London the plague could come knocking on every door in the street.

Life in the Middle Ages was an ideal breeding ground for disease – and London life, where families were packed together like sardines, without a nice field or wood to use as their toilet, was even dirtier.

Most families squashed in together in one smelly, filthy room. Often their pigs and chickens or cows might keep them company in the house. The mud floor would be covered with a greasy, slimy mess of scraps from the family dinner, decaying old bones, ancient straw, and assorted garbage. The roofs of their homes were made of mud and straw and the whole structure was made of wood. They didn't have toilets so they would use their living room as one! (Even the rich didn't mind pooing in the corner of their banqueting room and getting a serf to take it away!)

The homes of the Middle Ages may be awesomely gruesome by our standards but with all that wood, warm straw and comfy dirt they made great houses for rats and fleas. In fact, a rodent planning-committee couldn't have devised better homes.

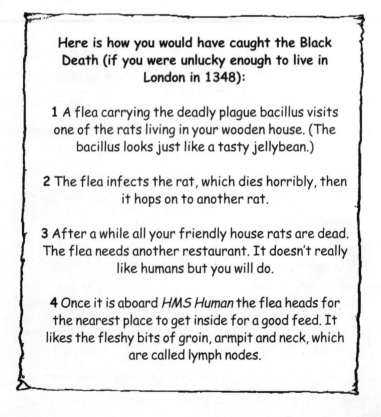

Here is how you would have caught the Black Death (if you were unlucky enough to live in London in 1348):

1 A flea carrying the deadly plague bacillus visits one of the rats living in your wooden house. (The bacillus looks just like a tasty jellybean.)

2 The flea infects the rat, which dies horribly, then it hops on to another rat.

3 After a while all your friendly house rats are dead. The flea needs another restaurant. It doesn't really like humans but you will do.

4 Once it is aboard *HMS Human* the flea heads for the nearest place to get inside for a good feed. It likes the fleshy bits of groin, armpit and neck, which are called lymph nodes.

So now you're a hotel-cum-restaurant for a vicious little tick. What are your chances?

1 You get a very high fever (105F), followed by aches, vomiting and convulsions.

2 Black boils appear in your groin, neck and armpits. These start off olive-sized, then they grow to the size of an egg. They can grow as large as an apple. Often you start coughing or sneezing.

3 These boils – or buboes – soon begin to spread all over your arms, thighs, legs and stomach.

4 The bubuoes begin oozing with blood and putrid pus.

5 You start letting off a real pong. Your breath, sweat and spit is so rancid your family can't be near you without the urge to vomit. Your wee forms a thick blackish red liquid.

6 You can start coughing up blood. This stage is pretty fatal and means the flea has injected the bacillus straight into your bloodstream. You are probably dead within three days. Often people became delirious and would perform a dance of death.

7 Sometimes hard shells form around the buboes. They begin to look a bit like bulbous beetles. This (despite all appearances) is a good sign. You might – just might – survive.

Here are some other medieval names for those yucky buboes – or 'rosies':

Knobs   **Kernels**   **Biles**   **Blaines**   **Blisters**   **Wheals**

Bubonic plague was bad, bad, bad. But our poor ancestors had something even worse to contend with: pneumonic plague. This plague appeared in cold weather when germs invaded the lungs. Victims coughed blood out through the nose and there was no hope – they would usually be dead within twenty-four hours.

As one gentleman put it, 'You could lunch with your family and dine with your maker (i.e. God).'

And what did the doctors do to stop the plague? A 101 things – but not one of them worked.

No one knew what caused the plague, least of all the doctors. Doctors wore long robes and masks with bronze beaks – sometimes with sweet-smelling herbs in the beak – to avoid catching it. One doctor even complained that the head-to-toe waxed robes he wore to keep infection off were useless as they only kept off the fleas! If only he had passed on his clothes rather than his medicine, more of his patients might have lived!

Some doctors refused to visit plague patients – giving all doctors a bad name. Not that the docs weren't having a hard time – their patients just kept dying on them. And it certainly wasn't money they were coughing up.

But doctors didn't let ignorance get in the way of their theories. They thought you could get plague from:

• Poisonous gases let off by the belly of the earth (Called miasma)

• Looking at an infected person (I wonder if these docs did their jobs without looking at their patients?)

• Dogs and cats (In London thousands of dogs and cats were rounded up and killed. There was even an official dog-killer. Unfortunately it meant that all the rats the cats and dogs might have killed were left scot-free.)

• Drinking from poisoned wells (Prejudice flourishes in times of fear and in many places they blamed Jews for poisoning the wells.)

• Some people thought the plague was God's vengeance for their wicked ways (People in those days never forgot to go to church.)

Mouldy Medieval Medicine

Imagine that you were a doctor in London in the 1300s and a young woman struck by plague was brought to you covered in swellings. Would you:

A) Wrap the patient in layers of cloth and shave the sign of the cross into her head.

B) Cover her buboes in treacle.

C) Spread a paste made out of honey, duck fat, turpentine, soot, treacle, egg yolks and scorpion oil onto the buboes.

D) Put a headless pigeon or chicken on her lower parts – to try to drain out the poison.

E) Tell her not to eat lettuce

F) Pray

G) All of the above

Answer: G) The doctors' cures were even crazier than their guesses about what caused the plague.

Here are some of their other crazy ideas:

The buboes were cut – to drain away bad blood – but patients simply died of shock. Cesspits were opened so that an even nastier smell would drive away the plague. Some people even sat in the cesspits!

People became obsessed with keeping the plague away. They would wear bracelets or lockets containing nasty poisonous things like arsenic, tin and mercury. The docs thought nasty things would attract other nasty things – because 'like attracts like'.

Superstitious people carried charms around with them, with the letters of the zodiac on them. One popular charm was the word ABRACADABRA, which was carried around on a slip of paper like this

```
A B R A C A D A B R A
 A B R A C A D A B R
  A B R A C A D A B
   A B R A C A D A
    A B R A C A D
     A B R A C A
      A B R A C
       A B R A
        A B R
         A B
          A
```

No one was safe from the Black Death – but it did seem to especially like the poor. This was partly because many rich Londoners and nobles escaped to their country homes as soon as the first whiff of plague struck.

Before they came back to town the rich would hire a fumigator who would smoke out their house with sulphur – this stank and didn't necessarily kill the fleas.

Some nastier nobles would even leave the maid in the house for a few weeks before they came back from the country – as a sort of human smoke alarm. If she died they'd know it wasn't safe to come back to London and they would spend a few more weeks in the country!

Many clergymen, monks and nuns died, although some bishops fled to their country homes. Some Londoners got really fed up with their poxy clergymen, who refused to visit the sick and dying to give them their last rites in case they caught the dreaded disease.

No wonder ordinary people were sick to what back teeth they had left after the plague had struck – and not just of the Black Death, but of their rotten nobles and clergy.

All over London, England and Europe the poor people realized that their lords were really a pretty good-for-nothing bunch. In some places they rebelled and refused to work as serfs. (Serfs were the property of their lord and had to do his 'bidding'. Mostly serfs were just bidden to work very, very, very hard.)

In 1381 English peasants revolted under the leadership of a man called Wat Tyler. The rebels assembled on Blackheath and marched on London, killing a lot of fat clerics and nobles on the way. They were let into the Tower of London by sympathizers where they murdered the hated Archbishop of Canterbury, Simon Sudbury, and many of his men. They cut off their heads and spiked them on the railings of London Bridge (I bet that stopped the Bish asking, 'What's that peasant chappie's name? Wat? Well that's a stupid name.')

But Wat didn't last much longer than his enemies. He was soon killed by the Lord Mayor of London, Sir William Walworth.

Rapping with your teacher

Here is a trick you can try out on your teacher. Say, 'Sir, Miss (or Mate, if you have a trendy teacher), can you tell me when rap started?' Your teacher will probably say, 'I don't have time for pop rubbish, Jones, or Smith, or Bottomley.' If you've got a hip teacher they might give you some spiel about rap starting as a sort of protest poetry in American ghettoes and add some stuff about Eminem and Puff Daddy.

You can then say, 'I'm afraid you're a few centuries out, Sir [or Miss or Jeff]. In the Middle Ages there were "plague raps".'

Then tell your teacher that the poor would dress up as skeletons and dance in graveyards, lit by flickering candles as they made up rhymes poking fun at all the big-shots who lorded it over them. They would remind people that nobles, bishops, kings and queens would all soon be just as dead, rotten and stinking as the peasants! The famous German painter Hans Holbein did a whole series of woodcuts showing death skeletons doing the danse macabre – the medieval tango. This is how a plague rap might go ... but you could always make up your own raps:

Look at you, you bag of bones
Once you sat on burnished thrones
You dined on larks and fancy treats
And now you're meat for worms to eat.

There was a time I called you lord,
I toiled for you, I feared your sword.
But Blackest Death, it takes no side
Rich and poor, no divide.

I may be hungry, but look at you,
Brains and guts for rats to chew.
I may be a serf, but I'm still well,
While you and yours are damned to hell.

CHAPTER TWO

The Great Plague of 1665

Bubonic plague had come back to visit London so many times it had become like the gatecrasher at parties everyone knows and nobody wants.

Since the first outbreak of bubonic plague in 1348 the Black Death had visited London seventeen times.

Over the centuries plague had become a business like any other. In times of plague there were thousands of Londoners who made their living (and too often their dying) out of those horrible buboes.

Let's take a trip down one typical London street – let's call it Pork and Pie Alley – to see what life would have looked like in the summer of 1665, the summer of the Great Plague of London.

Pork and Pie Alley is a close, packed warren of wooden houses. Rickety upper storeys hang over the pokey little lane, touching in the middle and cutting out sunlight. They look topsy-turvy, as if they could fall down at any moment.

In good times the gutter in the middle of the road runs with fresh sewage. This is a fast-food area where people often buy a slice of eel or lark pie for lunch and butchers chuck bone, gristle and other nasty things into the sewers. It is a crowded and noisy area, full of the bustle of carts and people going to market.

But these are bad times and the alley is deserted. All you can hear is the sad tolling of church bells – they ring for every death.

Walking down the street of fifteen houses you can see eight houses marked with big red crosses and the words Lord Have Mercy Upon Us. Outside these houses stands a watchman, covered from head to toe with greasy rags. He has covered his mouth and nose with grubby cotton – in a hopeless effort to ward off the plague - and is carrying a stout stick.

Eight whole families are imprisoned inside the houses with the cruel crosses on them. When anybody finds the tell-tale black rash upon their bodies (try as they might to hide it) their whole family are condemned. The familes that are jailed in their homes include those of Samuel Wood, the gravedigger, and Thomas Fenn, the blacksmith. These families fear a slow and lingering death – with the healthy catching the plague from the infected.

Samuel's job, digging huge pits for victims of the plague, brought him into daily contact with its horrors. Maybe knowing how he would end up made things worse. When he discovered the buboes on his skin he went out of his mind and ran naked into the street, foaming at the mouth. But the constable – his neighbour Luke Horne – caught him and shut him up in his house.

Now Samuel's wife Elizabeth and his eleven-year-old son John – the apple of his eye - have the horrible rash too. Samuel is in horrible pain from the excruciating boils all over his body. He no longer thinks much about what will happen to Lizzie and John, or to his five young daughters.

The fate of the eight condemned families in Pork and Pie Alley was typical of that suffered by poorer Londoners during the Great Plague.

The constable Luke Horne knows that shutting up his friend Samuel's healthy daughters with their sick dad is horribly cruel. But he is scared. He doesn't want his wife and baby son to die. He doesn't want to die himself.

Sometimes the wailing from his friend Samuel's house wakes Luke in the middle of the night.

But Luke doesn't know what else to do – so he does what the

government tells him to, however nasty the orders are.

The government has issued 'plague orders' which the individual parishes must put into action. Scared out of their wits that they might all die, people do as they are told. Often neighbours, like Luke and Samuel, would shut up their lifelong friends knowing they were condemning them to almost certain death.

Plague jobs were nasty and dangerous. They were usually done by the lowest of the low – as usual in times of pestilence most of the well off closed up their houses and fled to the country leaving the poor to fester and die in London.

King Charles II and his court escaped to Oxford. The House of Lords – also relatively safe in Oxford - only got around to debating the plague in the autumn. Their only two proposals were that no member of the Lords should be shut up in their houses and that no plague hospitals were built next to people of 'note and quality'.

The Mayor, Sir Thomas Bludworth, at least didn't run away from London when plague struck – he took the rather nutty course of sitting inside a glass cage for the entire time. He wouldn't speak to any visitors except through his cage.

Here are some of the jobs the lower orders (and a few brave others) did to try to stop the plague.

Pestilential Plague Jobs

Constables Had to report the number of deaths to the Mayor, shut up and mark infected houses and arrest wandering beggars. It was a dangerous job as constables could be attacked by plague-stricken maniacs – and if they neglected their duty they could be put in prison.

Examiners Had to carry a red stick when out in the streets. As senior officials, they had to discover infected houses and pay the wages of other plague officials.

Searchers Had to be 'honest and discreet matrons'. They took an oath that they would truthfully report every death to the constable. In fact, as no respectable woman would take such a dangerous job, like the viewers they were often poverty-stricken drunks.

Viewers Also old women, who had to report any infected person.

Watchmen Every infected house would have two watchmen armed with big sticks, one for the day and one for the night. Sometimes they would be bribed by the desperate people inside. Or people could try to escape by climbing out of windows and over roofs. Sometimes watchmen were killed so their prisoners could escape. The writer Daniel Defoe tells how one watchman was blown up with gunpowder.

Nurses Poor old women (again) who would care for the sick in the infected houses or in the very few plague hospitals. (They had a terrible reputation and were often accused of thieving – but given their dangerous job, can you blame them altogether?)

Bearers Carried red sticks and carted dead bodies to the grave. As they approached with their dead carts, they would ring their bells and cry out 'Cast out your dead'. They could make good money as they were often paid for every body they buried.

Gravediggers The lowest of the low, who buried the bodies in the plague pits.

Londoners shut up thousands of families in their homes (there was only one rebellion in Covent Garden). But it was no use. The plague killed thousands and then tens of thousands – so many that their bodies were covered in quicklime or rough sheets and tossed into huge plague pits. One of these pits – the Great Pit – is under Aldgate. Next time you walk there remember the thousands of bones you're cruising over.

Desperate times drove men to desperate acts. Wild ideas and beliefs of all kinds flourished. People claimed to see fiery angels in the sky, blazing comets or hearses and coffins travelling through the air. Daniel Defoe, in his book *A Journal of The Plague Year*, tells of the 'famous Solomon Eagle' who went about stark naked with a pan of burning charcoal on his head, begging, 'Spare us, good Lord, spare thy people'.

But then as an unusually harsh winter drew in, the plague died out as suddenly as it had erupted. Slowly the clergy, the nobles and the rich folk trickled back to the great city – after making sure their homes and streets were fumigated.

King Charles II took his time coming home, finally returning to London in the next year, 1666. His mucky court left behind a real tip in the Oxford college they'd camped out in: 'excrements in every corner in chimneys, studies, coal houses, cellars.'

The passing of the Great Plague left behind a shattered city. At least 68,000 people had died, one in every six Londoners. Everyone had lost someone ... husbands, brothers, sisters, children, friends ...

Life still had to go on in the scarred city and it did. But life was never the same again. There was a shortage of people, which meant that workmen could demand better wages and the wealthy were forced to pay them. (This happened in other great attacks of plague too.)

Some people even believe that the plague changed our notion of TIME itself. (Not in a super-brainy Einstein type way.) The plague replaced a slowish, leisurely world where time was calculated according to harvests and marriages and funerals with one where it was all snap and go. There weren't enough people to go around, so plague survivors had to learn how to hurry.

Merchant time calculated life according to the tick-tock of the watch. Minutes, even seconds, started to matter. Gone was the old dawdling life where 11 o'clock was pretty much the same as 12 o'clock.

So the next time your mum nags you've got five minutes to brush your teeth and get into bed – you'll realize that you have the bubonic plague to blame.

Smoking out the Plague

People were frantic to try and stop the plague. They checked their bodies every day for the rash – as your mum might check your hair for lice. Schoolboys at Eton College were even caned if they refused to do something. Was this:

A) To drink their own wee for breakfast?

B) To chant Abracadabra and dance naked five times round a burning fire every morning?

C) To smoke tobacco?

D) To chant the Lord's prayer 1665 times a day?

Answer C) Forget Harry Potter or Playstation - smoking, which people believed helped keep the plague away, was the craze of the day. Eton schoolboys who refused to smoke were beaten very nastily. Some people took chain-smoking to new extremes, always having a lighted fag to hand. Other people even slept with a wad of chewing tobacco in their mouth.

CHAPTER THREE

The Great Fire

London after the Great Plague was a sad city. It was hard to get away from so many deaths.

But it was also starting to come to life again. The streets were crowded with fishmongers and barrow boys, calling their wares. Fresh, pongy sewage again flowed in the centre of the road.

People thought the Bad Times were over. But have you ever heard the expression it never rains but it pours? Because plague-ridden London was now to be visited by the equivalent of a flood. (Actually considering the trouble in store they could have done with a bit of rain.)

It all started with a batch of burnt bread. Here is what the local newspaper had to say about it in the week of 3 September, 1666:

The London Gazette

At one of the Clock in the morning, there hapned to break out a sad and deplorable Fire in Pudding Lane, neer New Fish street, which falling at that hour of the night, and in quarter of town so close built with wooden pitch houses spread itself so far before day ... that the lamentable fire in a short time became too big to be mastred.

(Hmm, whoever wrote that obviously got bottom marks in spelling! And hadn't they heard of a FULL STOP in 1666?)

Anyway the fire started in the shop of Thomas Farynor, the king's baker. His assistant awoke and found that the house was full of smoke and roused his master. Everyone escaped but the maid – who was too scared to climb out of the window and over the roofs – instead the poor girl burnt to death.

The fire loved the tar that held the houses together and soon it spread far and wide. If the Mayor, Sir Thomas Bludworth, had ordered wooden houses in the fire's path to be pulled down right away, the fire might have run out of things to burn and been stopped. But he didn't get it right. When Sir Thomas was woken up and told the city was on fire, he thought it was just another minor blaze and went back to bed complaining, 'A woman might piss it out.'

Within hours whole streets, then districts were alight. (The mayor, silly man, was at his wit's end. He complained: 'Lord what can I do? … People will not obey me' … but what could you expect

31

of a man who spent the Great Plague talking to people through a glass cage?)

The best witness of the fire was a man called Samuel Pepys who watched it from a nice, safe spot across the Thames and said it was 'A most malicious bloody flame, as one entire arch of fire ... of above a mile long.

Pepys' Deadly Diaries

Samuel Pepys was an important man, a naval official who had the King's ear. (No, he didn't carry around the king's ear – this means the King listened to him) He loved the good life: pretty ladies, fine wines and cheese and he also loved his faithful wife Elizabeth (though that didn't stop lusty Pepys chasing other wenches).

Pepys had stayed in London through most of the plague – though he had sent his wife and children away. This was odd because he was a bit of a hypochondriac (i.e. someone who thinks they've got every disease in the medical dictionary). If he wasn't complaining about his gout he was going on about his piles. Indeed every year he had a party to celebrate an operation to remove a stone in his bladder. (How do you fancy celebrating having your tonsils out instead of your birthday?)

Pepys is famous today because he kept diaries. Hundreds and hundreds of pages of them. Pages about everything he did and all the great events of his age. The strange thing was that Pepys wrote them in code called tachygraphy – and they weren't decoded for hundreds of years.

When Pepys heard about the fire he immediately buried his most precious things. No, not his wife – his parmesan cheese and his wine! This is what he said about the fire:

"Poor people staying in their houses as long as till the very fire touched them, and then running into boats, or clambering from one pair of stairs by the waterside to another. And among other things, the poor pigeons, I perceive, were loth to leave their houses, but hovered about the windows, and balconies, till some of them burned their wings and fell down."

Pepys wrote his diary in code because he wanted to keep his secrets from the prying eyes of his wife. But you could make up your own version of tachygrapy and write your own secret diary.

Within five days one and a half miles of the city lay in ashes. It burnt down 89 churches and over 13,000 houses. About 80 per cent of the city was aflame. But strangely only six people were known to have died.

Among other things it burnt down the pub that the playwrights William Shakespeare and Ben Jonson used to have their ale in. (Perhaps Shakespeare would have said it was all

Much Ado About Nothing.)

Thousands of people saw everything they owned go up in smoke. The homeless lived in tent cities for months, even years, afterwards.

But there were some people who saw the fire as a chance to make a bit of dough (no, not more bread, money – or bung as it was called then). One of them was the architect Christopher Wren. He sent King Charles II a plan of how he wanted to rebuild the city. The King liked the grand plans very much – but wondered who would pay for it. The King certainly wasn't planning to out of his own pocket.

Instead Wren built St Paul's cathedral. And he also designed a monument to the fire (it's on Monument Street, of course). This is a column 202 feet high – and exactly 202 feet from the baker's shop. At first the monument was meant to have a statue of the king on it. But he declined the honour, fearing that it would only make people think of his uselessness in failing to stop the fire. So Wren replaced the King's head with a bowl of flames.

The fire, as the diary writer John Evelyn said, was a 'miserable and calamitous spectacle'. But there are some clever historians who say it was a good thing. Was this:

A) Because it gave builders a lot of work?

B) It destroyed lots of wood and straw houses?

C) London was so dirty the best thing to do was to burn it down?

D) Some barrels full of powder exploded during the fire, leading to the invention of gunpowder?

Answer: B) Those wood and straw houses were the ideal homes for plague-carrying rats. These houses were then largely rebuilt in brick and stone. Some people think that the plague vanished from England after the Great Fire because those lovely rodent homes had gone! (Others think it is because the plague-carrying black house rat disappeared and was replaced by the brown sewer rat ...)

If you have trouble remembering boring old dates this handy rhyme will help:

In 1665 no one was left alive
In 1666 London was burnt to sticks

In 1986 the Baker's Company finally said sorry for causing the Great Fire. Honestly. Try it yourself: 'Don't hassle me, Mum. I'll apologize for burning down the garden shed when I'm 320.'

Chapter Four

Dangerous Doctors

'Trust me, I'm a doctor.' There's something comforting about these words, isn't there? I don't know about you, but when I'm sick I always feel a bit better when I've been to the doctor.

But how would you feel if the doctor thought that your chickenpox was caused by the smell in your room? Or because God was angry that you hadn't done your homework? What if the doctor suggested applying some live leeches to your spots?

You'd be terrified, wouldn't you? I would be. Scared silly. And more of the nutty doctor than the illness itself.

The docs in London's history – right up till the 1850s, when things began to really change – had no remedies for most of the nasty plagues and pestilences in this book. And, believe me, live leeches weren't as horrid as some of their other so-called 'cures'.

Surgeons (or 'sawbones' as they were nicknamed – no prizes for guessing why) worked with saws, axes, pliers and other things that are now builders' tools. If they didn't like the look of something they cut it off. One of their favourite operations was trepanning – or boring a hole in the patient's skull – if it didn't kill the poor patient it might just cure them!

Sawbones didn't use painkillers either. This is partly because they weren't yet invented. But maybe our ancestors just got used to horrendous, excruciating pain because for some reason surgeons didn't much use opium and the other knock-outs that they did have.

In fact doctors were a bit useless in how they diagnosed - or detected - disease. Their treatments were usually based on the idea of helping nature by forcing out evil gases – which they called 'humours'. Disease, they believed, was caused by the things turning putrid and nasty inside the body – whether blood, urine, sweat, gases and so on.

Their so-called cures were based on the idea of getting as many of these rotten things out of the body as possible. This, as you can imagine, made for some very violent treatments - like cutting open a vein to draw out blood, or making the patient massively sweat or vomit. Perhaps nastiest of all was the habit of putting a tube up the backside and pumping water through to remove the contents of the tummy and bowels – called an enema.

Ode to the Enema

In 1719 Edward Baynard, a London doctor, summed up the practice of medicine:

For in some ten words the whole art is comprised;

For some of the ten are always advised

Piss, Spew and Spit

Perspiration and Sweat

Purge, Bleed and Blister

Issues and Clyster

(Issues are discharges from the skin, Purge meant vomiting and Blister was the habit of putting small heated cups on the skin till it blistered, then pricking the blisters till they bled. Clysters meant enemas. This sort of violent blistering and bleeding was sometimes called heroic medicine – but little wonder that patients didn't want to call their 'heroic' doctors till they were half-dead.

The theories and the practice of old-fashioned docs were a disaster - they didn't think of looking at all the cases of the plague or typhoid, for example, and trying to figure out what they had in common. Because the churches thought it was bad to cut up humans in order to find out what had caused disease, doctors based their theories on the bodies of animals.

The Greek doctor Galen (who was around in AD 131 and was a doctor to the gladiators) was the expert most London doctors referred to before the 1700s. He grumbled that a doc without human bodies to cut up was like an architect without a plan – but he was forced to 'prove' his theories on the bodies of apes and pigs. (Herophilus, the founder of the Alexandria medical school in 332 BC had the answer: he cut up criminals from the royal jails – while the poor wretches were still alive!)

Many of the doctors who gave out pills and potions before modern medicine changed everything were good and honest – but some were also frauds and quacks. The good men didn't know they were useless. The quacks – whose name comes from the word Quacksalver or salve (ointment) seller - might have had an inkling that the potions they sold were rubbish.

Quack, Quack, I'm a Doctor

Here are some medicines that quacks and doctors claimed would cure you. See if you can match the disease with the cure. But don't try to imagine eating the peacock pooh with slimy snails ... some things are *tooooo* horrible to imagine.

A] Peacock dung with snail

B] Powdered roast mouse

C] Cow dung fried in butter

D] Leeches

E] Electricity

F] Small heated cups applied to patients – the blisters caused would open and bleed

G] Surgical vest that sucked the disease from the body

H] Celestial (heavenly) beds connected to electrical currents

I] Swallowing a glass of the urine of a healthy person

J] Applying live earthworms to affected areas till they begin to stink

K] Blow-dried human pooh in the eye

1. To cure consumption

2. To cure a sore breast

3. To cure piles (a nasty complaint affecting the bottom area!)

4. To suck flu from the body

5. Almost anything

6. To cure not being able to control when you need to go to the toilet

7. To cure paralysis and palsy (the shakes)

8. To cure women who couldn't have babies

9. To cure cataract (a film over the eyes)

10. To cure fits

11. To cure gout

The answers are A1) B6) C2) D3) E7) F5) G4) H8) I10) J11) K9)

41

Some of these cures could be applied to more than one illness. But in the end it doesn't matter which pairs you matched up. They're all pretty useless anyway! Other cures which were more likely to kill were 'fustigation' (the poor patient was actually given a beating), and tonic made from ground-up human skull!

One of the ways docs pulled the wool over people's eyes was the language they used. This is how Henry Fielding poked fun at the habit in his novel *Tom Jones*:

'I was once I remember' (said the surgeon) 'called to a patient who received a violent contusion in his tibia by which the exterior cutis was lacerated, so that there was profuse sanguinary discharge; and the interior membranes were so divellicated that the os or bone very plainly appeared through the aperture of the vulnus or wound ... Some febril symptoms intervening at the time (for the pulse was exuberant and indicated some phlebotomy.'

Doctors still sometimes talk mumbo-jumbo! Translated into plain English the surgeon is saying that he was called to see a man who had cut his leg so badly that the bone was showing, and that he had lost blood and had a high temperature!

Have you ever noticed how people who want to impress often use much more complicated language than is necessary? Next time you want to show off your cleverness, why not write in your own 'medical language' ... along the lines of: 'Dear Sir, I can't come to lessons today because I've got rheumatic divellications of the os or bone and sanguinary febril symptoms'.

The quacks had even more fun than the docs. They would set up stall in a market – sometimes with jugglers or monkeys or conjurers – and attract large crowds with their boasts of a miracle cure. Sometimes they would invite members of the crowd (who were in their pay) on to the platform – and 'cure' them of blindness or fevers or a broken leg.

Some quacks claimed that one 'universal medicine' would cure everything. George Jones, who made the 'Friendly Pill' in the 1680s, for example, claimed it would cure 'Pains in the Head, Face, Nose, Shoulders, Arms, Back, Breast, Belly, Thighs ... consumption, fevers ...' (I've cut the list down a bit because it goes on and on.)

The Pisse Prophets

Pee-gazing or 'uroscopy' was a type of 'medicine' that had come down from the mouldy Middle Ages. Pisse prophets would gaze at a sick person's urine and then tell them what was wrong with them.  (I wonder why no one set up business as a pooh prophet or a dung doctor?) By 1770 most doctors had decided that pee-gazing was rubbish!

But pee-gazing could still make you rich!

One of the most famous uroscopists in London in 1770 was called Theodor Myersbach. 'Doctor' Myserbach was a German post office clerk who came to London and tried to join the circus as a horse rider (he was turned down because he was too short). Instead he took to medicine and, without any training of any kind, grew rich enough to buy a house in posh Soho.

He became a very rich doctor with famous clients and boasted that he could tell the age, sex and life story of the patient just by looking at their pee. People loved the Doc's wicked potions, particularly the one that contained opium and alcohol and was strong enough to knock out a horse. Another potion was just water in which toast had been soaked!

Then a reporter from the *Gazetteer* newspaper went to see the great con artist with a flask full of horse wee. Doc Myersbach claimed to see that it was a 'lady's water'. This is a bit of his conversation with the reporter disguised as a patient:

Patient: What do you think is her complaint, Doctor?

Doctor: It be, Sir – it be a disorder in her womb – her womb – her- her womb be somewhat affected.

Patient: The water seems very clear, Doctor, doesn't it?

Doctor: Ah! Ah! It looks so to you: but I do see a slime upon the kidneys. She be very sick at the stomach – she have a pain in her head and in her limbs. Has she had many children?

Amazingly even after this was printed in the newspapers some people still went to see the phony doc. They claimed all newspapers were full of lies anyway.

Londoners were so used to quacks and frauds of all kinds that even a blatant phoney like Myersbach still had many people believing in him. But gradually – in the period after 1810 – a huge change in the way doctors worked came about. For a start they began to look at the patient to see what was wrong – rather than only putting their trust in God or doctors like Hippocrates, who worked a long, long time ago, in around 400 BC.

Saviours of Science

Around the time the little Emperor Napoleon was going around starting wars all over the place (1803–15) another Frenchman, called René Laennec, began to do something much more worthwhile. He listened very carefully to what he heard in a patient's chest and then compared it with the corpse of the patient after they died.

By doing this he was able to match, for example, the puffing sound someone with the white death (tuberculosis) makes with the appearance of their chest after death. A new science called pathology (which involves lots of cutting up of dead bodies) was born.

The second huge advance was the germ theory of disease. This was based on the idea that germs (not God or gases or miasma) caused disease. A German doctor called Robert Koch caused a huge sensation when he proved in 1876 that a bacteria caused tuberculosis (he had seen it under his microscope). It was a sensation! Gone were centuries of believing in miasma and gases, and other fanciful theories. Suddenly scientists raced to find the germs that caused typhoid, cholera, measles and all the other horrid diseases that affected humans.

These pioneering docs changed medicine from being a thing of hocus pocus and roasted snails to the modern science it is today.

They are also the reason why you and I don't don't dive out the nearest window when the doc comes calling ...

CHAPTER FIVE

Chronic Cholera

Victorian London was the biggest and richest city anyone had ever seen – almost the capital of the world. Victorians boasted that the sun never set on the British Empire – and they were right.

From the Sahibs [bosses] of India to the Massahs [bosses] of Nigeria to the Poms [bosses] of Australia, there was always a Brit cracking the whip as someone else slaved away.

Fine Victorian ladies and gentlemen sped around London in splendid carriages, on roads lit by glowing gas lights. They wore silks and calico from India and feasted off porcelain from China.

The city was growing at a huge rate, gobbling up green fields and forests as it grew fatter. It was full of landlords and labourers, clerks and cabbies, fancy ladies and fraudsters. Hoardes of peasants flocked to it every day.

They dreamt of streets paved with gold.

'London is more than a city; it is a whole kingdom in itself,' is how the writer Sidney Webb put it in 1891. 'The three next largest cities in the world could almost be combined without outnumbering its millions.'

But do you think that London's power and glory meant it was no longer foul, fetid, filthy and festering?

Think again.

Travellers riding to the capital in the 1850s were warned of the city's approach by the stink. And then there was the fog – thick, yellowish-black, very, very smelly. Sometimes it was impossible to see your feet because the fog was so thick. Even if you wrote a letter indoors on a winter's morning you would need to light a candle to see the paper clearly. (What a great excuse for bunking off your homework. 'Sorry, Miss, I couldn't see my notebook.')

Diseases ran through the population like a hungry tiger runs through a pack of big game hunters ...

The lives of children had not improved much since the Middle Ages. They were sent out to work as chimney sweeps or to slave away in factories. If the little sweep died from coal poisoning, or from suffocating in the chimney, the master sweep would simply buy another 'apprentice' from the workhouse.

Imagine you were a child born of a labourer in East London's Bethnal Green in 1830. You were living in the heart of the greatest empire known to man. To what age do you think you could hope to live?
A) 85 **B)** 2 **C)** 60 **D)** 16 **E)** 35

Answer : D

So for all its grandness Victorian London was really a pretty dirty and unhealthy sort of place – at least for the poor.

But both the rich and the poor were terrified of disease rushing through the packed and dirty city. And cholera more than lived up to their worst fears.

THE LONDON CHOLERA NEWS

13 February 1831

A new plague has visited our nation. The dreaded cholera morbus has sailed into London on the boats from India. On the way it has also struck at Persia, Russia and our German cousins.

We wait in fear for this evil visitation. The government has ordered a national day of prayer and fasting to beg for God's mercy.

Ships sailing from Germany are to be quarantined for eleven days near Deptford in East London. Doctors will check all sailors and crewmen to make sure they are free of the dreaded cholera before they are allowed on solid land.

But, alas, we fear that the government is not telling us the whole truth. The plague is already with us. A seaman has already died of the cholera. And yesterday a raker of wood and scrap from the Thames, Sarah Ferguson, was struck down. Unconfirmed reports say her limbs had turned blue in death – a sure sign of asiatic cholera.

We warn our readers that the disease strikes like lightning. First come loose motions, then cramps, vomiting, fever, death. It is said by observers of the disease in foreign lands that a boy can eat his breakfast, hale and hearty, and yet be buried in the evening.

London went into a panic as the disease spread. People stopped going to the theatre and vicars noticed their sermons suddenly became very unpopular. The Marquis of Stafford wouldn't even let the postman in and had his letters thrown into his house.

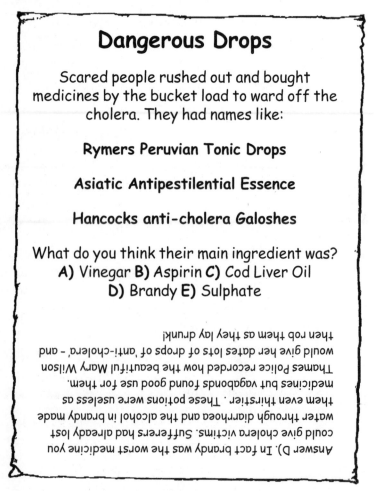

Dangerous Drops

Scared people rushed out and bought medicines by the bucket load to ward off the cholera. They had names like:

Rymers Peruvian Tonic Drops

Asiatic Antipestilential Essence

Hancocks anti-cholera Galoshes

What do you think their main ingredient was?
A) Vinegar **B)** Aspirin **C)** Cod Liver Oil
D) Brandy **E)** Sulphate

Answer D). In fact brandy was the worst medicine you could give cholera victims. Sufferers had already lost water through diarrhoea and the alcohol in brandy made them even thirstier. These potions were useless as medicines but vagabonds found good use for them. Thames Police recorded how the beautiful Mary Wilson would give her dates lots of drops of 'anti-cholera' - and then rob them as they lay drunk!

Apart from announcing their day of prayer and fasting, the government was clueless. (The poor who didn't have enough food anyway weren't very keen on the fasting idea.)

When people started dropping like flies during 1832 local councils did set up some special hospitals. Many normal hospitals wouldn't accept cholera patients - in case they infected other patients.

Doctors were not trusted much either. When two women from Mile End Old Town in East London caught cholera they thought their doctor's medicine was making them feel worse (I wonder if it had brandy in it?). Their friends fed some to their cat. When their cat died, the friends attacked the  doctors. When other members of the family later became ill, they refused to go to hospital.

People were also scared of going to hospital because there was a major shortage of corpses for medical students to practise on. (Advances in medicine meant that corpses were in great demand for doctors to prove their theories on and students to learn about human anatomy.) Grave-robbers and bodysnatchers flourished! Rumours spread that poor people were taken to cholera hospitals and killed so their bodies could be cut up.

These rumours were untrue. But there were cases of body-snatchers stealing the bodies of cholera victims – and of empty coffins being buried.

Lots and lots of Londoners died of cholera in the 1832 epidemic – at least 3000 – and then it suddenly went away as swiftly as it had come.

The next time it really hit London badly was 1854, and again the government and the medical profession were unprepared. Doctors still thought cholera was spread by the rotten gases (called miasma) in the air. No one had really thought of studying the cholera patients to see if, for example, they had all drunk the same dirty water.

But one man – John Snow, cholera detective – was on the case.

John Snow was the doctor who had delivered Queen Victoria's babies. But what really interested him was epidemiology (how diseases are spread).

When cholera hit Broad Street in Soho – in what Snow called 'the most terrible outbreak' the country had ever seen – the reaction was panic amongst rich and poor alike. People fled their homes and business. Within three days twelve people, living in or near the street, had died.

It was like the Black Death all over again.

Snow had done some research and was convinced that cholera was spread by dirty, infected water – and London water was horribly dirty.

He decided to prove his theory so he walked all around Soho, interviewing the families of cholera victims.

Again and again he found that they had drunk the water from a pump in Broad Street. No one believed him – not the water company, or the local councillors. They pointed out that there were deaths from cholera that didn't seem to be linked to the Broad Street pump – like that of a widow who lived in Hampstead.

Dr Snow rode up to Hampstead and found out that the widow – who had once lived in Broad Street – liked the taste of Soho water so much that she sent her servant down every day in a cart to bring back a large bottle for her.

Talk about a deadly brew!

Finally the powers that be snapped the handle off the pump.

With the death toll standing at 616 in Soho - suddenly cholera all but vanished.

But there were some who still didn't believe Snow. Local vicar Henry Whitehead believed it was all down to the wrath of God (that old chestnut). He did his own research and lo and behold he found Snow was right.

The vicar even found where it had all probably started.

Just before the epidemic a tiny baby living at 40 Broad Street had caught cholera. Its dirty nappies were soaked in water. The water was thrown into a cesspool which leaked into the water coming out of the Broad Street pump.

Detective Snow had caught his bug. But even though Snow was Queen Vic's pet doctor the water companies still didn't clean up their act – and many people still didn't believe that infected water spread cholera.

Where is your proof? they cried to Snow.

So people still continued to die from cholera.

Wicked Water

What finally proved that cholera is transmitted by infected water?

A) The Queen's tenth child died of cholera and doctors cut out and examined its stomach

B) The cholera bacteria was spotted under a microscope

C) There were a thousand more cases and it was proved they all used the same well

Answer: B) Though Snow had seen white wriggly things in the Broad Street water he couldn't prove they caused cholera. German Scientist Robert Koch had a better microscope and he found the little comma-shaped bacillus that caused cholera. In 1876 he finally proved that bugs in dirty water spreads cholera.

Today we have clean running water and cholera has vanished from London. But in developing countries, where basics like clean water are still a dream for many millions of people, a glass of water can still be a carrier of death by cholera.

CHAPTER SIX

The Great Stink

A walk down medieval Watling Street was more of a test of courage and skill than any of Lara Croft's cyber-battles.

For one thing there was the stink – a foul perfume of human and animal sewage, urine, rotting fish bones and anything else disgusting you'd care to think of! (A 21st-century time traveller would have to go around with a scented handkerchief to their nose. And remember the stinky dirt wasn't just smelly – it created the right home for foul diseases of all kinds.)

Houses were built so that their upper floors hung over the street, closing in all the foul smells and cutting out fresh air and sunlight.

Then there was no knowing when the lady of the house would fling out garbage on to the street. Sometimes a passser-by in the street would have the revolting contents of a chamberpot emptied on their heads.

Eurgh. And we complain about the odd pigeon!

Finally, one false step and you could land in the sewers that flowed merrily through the centre of big streets and down the sides of small ones.

The sewers weren't meant to contain anything too solid but Jonathan Swift, the author of Gullivers Travels wrote that they were often chock-a-block with:

Sweepings from butcher's stalls, Dung, Guts, and blood, drowned puppies, stinking sprats and drenched in mud, dead cats and turnip tops until a shower of rain mercifully shifted the contents towards the Thames.

London was a diabolically dirty place. The typical London family lived in a one-room slum with their animals, never took a bath, and rarely washed their bug-infested clothes. Indeed Queen Elizabeth I, who insisted on four baths a year, was thought to be the cleanest woman in London.

Just (Foul) Jobs:

Nightsoil men removed the human and and animal dung from the putrefying cesspits under houses and took it away to sell to farmers for manure. (Nightsoil was a polite word for pooh.) Gong Fermor was another name for a nightsoil man.

Rakers were paid by each ward in the city to rake through the sewers and remove the slops in a wheelbarrow.

Toshers looked in the sewers for bits of string, coins, metal, anything that they could sell.

Mudlarks were children who scraped the mud of the Thames river for bits of coal

Dredgers searched the Thames for dead bodies.

It wasn't cheap to get a nightsoil man in to clean your cesspit regularly, so the tight-fisted or poor just let the mess grow and grow and grow ... On 20 October 1660 Samuel Pepys (him again) wrote angrily in his diary about the day his neighbour's cesspit overflowed: 'Going down to my cellar ... I put my feet into great heaps of turds.' (Hmm, for sheer nastiness, those cesspit rows must beat arguments about the garden fence falling over.)

Sometimes smart alecks would come up with schemes to pipe their waste into their neighbours' houses. Two men were actually put on trial in 1347 for a nifty plan to pipe their stinky sewage into their neighbour's cellar – nobody noticed till it had started to overflow .

Overflowing sewers and cesspits weren't just smelly – they often leaked into nearby rivers and wells which was very, very dangerous during times of pestilence.

People were getting angry that London was so stinky. In 1349, during the Black Death, even King Edward III got in on the act. He wrote a letter to complain to the mayor which said:

Dear Mayor

The streets and lanes through which people have to pass are foul with human faeces [pooh] and the air of the city poisoned to the great danger of people passing. Especially in this time of infectious disease.

[i.e. do something about it!]

By order of
The King

And do you know what the cheeky mayor replied? He said that he couldn't do anything about it because all the rakers were dead of the plague.

But it wasn't as if people in the Dark Ages (circa 400–1000) or the relatively modern Middle Ages (circa 1000 to 1500) didn't notice how filthy things were: all sorts of Londoners, kings, queens and mayors, as well as common folk, kept trying to get the city to clean up its act.

One of them was the most famous Lord Mayor of London, Dick Whittington (the one with the cat). Whittington, who died in 1423, built the first public lavatories – really just holes over cesspits – and passed a law that promised to punish anyone that cast dung or garbage into the road.

A Pile of Old Pooh

The price of nightsoil went up as gong fermors found a new market for old pooh in the 1500s. Did they sell it to:

A) Gunpowder men who extracted nitrogen from it?

B) Early make-up artists who extracted potash from it for use in beauty treatment masks for rich ladies?

Answer A) There was a booming business extracting nitrogen from pooh to make gunpowder for the wars that Queen Elizabeth was fighting against the Spanish.

By Victorian times cesspits were a real menace and the reformer Edwin Chadwick spoke of visiting houses where the cellars were permanently blocked by (I'm being polite) nightsoil. In other houses people had to walk over bricks to their gate because the front gardens were always six inches deep in ... errrm ... nightsoil.

If you thought you could wash away the stink – forget it. Water was far too precious.

Families had to lug their water from wells or rivers – sometimes miles away. These wells are remembered in modern names such as Clerks Well or Clerkenwell and Wells Court near St Pauls. Richer people could have their water delivered in a cart.

Foul Facts

• During the great famines before the Black Death first hit London people were so hungry they ate pigeon's droppings, nettles, dung and even the flesh of executed thieves and murderers.

• While the poor starved the rich ate and ate ... A good dinner for an aristocrat in the 1700s would start at 3pm, last for four hours and include about 30 dishes, such as pie with partridge, quail and larks or roast swan. The meal went on for so long chamber pots were placed in the corners of the hall. The French traveller André Parreaux wrote: 'The person who has occasion to use it does not even interrupt his talk during the operation.'

• In 1326 Richard the Raker fell into

a cesspit and
'drowned
monstrously in
his own
excrement'.

• Housewives stored urine till it was very strong ... it
could be used as a cheap (if smelly) bleach to remove
the stains from dirty clothes.

By 1810 the huge expansion of London was literally bathing the
city in its own nightsoil. There were about two hundred
thousand sewers for a population of a million. Forty years later,
when the population was close on three million, the problems
were even worse.

Funnily enough, it was a big improvement – the invention of
the water closet (now you know what WC stands for) – which
finally made the sewers crack up.

The first (very basic) flush toilets were installed in Richmond at
the palace of Queen Elizabeth I in the 1590s but it wasn't till well
over 200 years later that they took off. One of the men who made a
mint of money from those posh new toilets in 1861 was Thomas
Crapper (who gave four letters of his name to a substance often
found in his WCs). His flash porcelain flush handles were advertised

with the slogan, 'A Certain Flush with every Pull'.

By Victorian times thousands of WCs were emptying their contents into improved drains that, unfortunately, dumped directly into the rivers. Meanwhile water was pumped from the rivers back into improved street pumps and the taps that richer people had put in their houses.

No wonder people got sick. Cholera, dysentery, typhoid – all these diseases are passed from sick people into sewage and then back into drinking water. 'He who drinks a tumbler [glass] of London water' – the society gentlemen Sydney Smith told Lady Grey in 1834 – 'has literally more animated beings in his stomach than there are men, women and children on the face of the globe.'

The Great Stink

Even when Dr Snow, the bug detective, pointed out the connection between dirty water and thousands of cholera deaths no one really took any notice. It was something else that finally persuaded the important people to build a new sewage system for London. Was it:

A) Queen Victoria caught cholera from a cup of tea made with water from the Thames?

B) A hot dry summer caused the smell from the sewage-filled Thames to become so strong that Parliament had to be closed down.

C) Heavy rains made the Thames overflow, causing raw sewage to flood the streets and run into Buckingham Palace Gardens?

ANSWER B) In the boiling summer of 1858, hot weather made the stench from the Thames so pongy that the windows of Parliament had to be hung with sheets soaked in chloride of lime (even pongier cleaning stuff). The press called the whole thing 'The Great Stink' and panicked members of parliament fled the buildings. No surprises that soon after, a law was passed granting pots of money to the engineer Sir Joseph Bazalgette to really sort out London's disgusting drains. His grand system of 1300 miles of main sewers abolished the stinky cesspit and still exists today!

Water was more tricky to sort out than sewage because there were nine water companies that drew the foul brew – by now a brown sludge – from the Thames and sold it to Londoners. One company even drew its water from a point next to the Great Ranelagh Sewer – one of the biggest sewers in London! These companies didn't want to waste money on cleaning and filtering. But it wasn't just the poor who suffered the consequences.

In 1861 Queen Victoria's beloved husband Prince Albert caught typhoid and died. His wife was inconsolable. She wore black for the rest of her life and kept his room exactly the

66

same. She even had servants bring up 'Bertie's' water for him to shave every morning.

Typhoid is a horrible disease – spread by dirty water and milk. The sufferer catches very high fever and death can follow quickly. Ten years after her husband's death Queen Vic's oldest son Edward also caught the disease and was on the verge of death.

The typhoid was said to come from dirty water in the newly installed WC and a plumber was called in to fix the problem. Edward was very grateful and posh people began to take more care of personal hygiene (i.e. they started to have weekly rather than yearly baths) and to boil their water.

Now, of course, Londoners take clean water and hidden drains for granted. But these basic things that keep our city clean in fact save more lives than any number of pills and potions. Sadly clean water is not available everywhere. In some countries thousands of children still get typhoid and cholera from dirty water.

CHAPTER SEVEN

The Speckled Monster

Lo the Smallpox with horrid glare

Levelled its terrors at the fair;

And, rifling every youthful grace,

Left but the remnant of a face .

Oliver Goldsmith, 1760

By the 1800s the slums in East and South London had become so rotten that the smell had even started to waft down to the posh West End of town. (Your parents probably tell you your room is a slum if there are a few crisp packets on the floor. They ain't seen nothing. They should take a trip to a real slum.)

Wealthy Victorians were forced to notice the stench of the slums because these foul places bred diseases – which they could catch just as easily as the poor. They called these places 'fever nests'.

One of the greatest slum pestilences was smallpox – feared as much as the Black Death for the yucksome sores that erupted all over a sufferer's body. Smallpox survivors ended up with skin as pebbly as an orange – and with gruesome scars. Often they would go blind and end up horribly disfigured. No wonder the disease was called the Speckled Monster.

Smallpox could spread like wildfire and, worse, it could kill in 48 hours.

Charles the Cheerful

Charles Dickens – who your teachers will tell you was a great writer – was certainly different from most other Victorian do-gooders. Dicken's father had been thrown into Marshalsea Prison in London because he couldn't pay his debts. At the age of twelve Dickens was forced to go to work in Warren's Blacking Factory in Hungerford, labelling bottles.

Dickens never got over all the awful things he saw as child. He knew the terrible things that went on in London.

In *Bleak House*, one of his greatest (and unfortunately longest) books, he blasted the Victorian public with a scary description of the rookeries – and told them the dreadful diseases that bred there wouldn't stay out of sight in the slums. Diseases would creep out in the water and air and kill off the better sort too. He was right: lots of nobles and even royals, such as

Mary II, who ruled from 1689 to 1694, died of smallpox. Dickens called his slum Tom-all-alone but it was very similar to slums that posh Londoners hurried past with hankies over their noses – like St Giles in what is now Covent Garden.

'There is not an atom of Tom's slime,' Dickens writes cheerfully, 'not a cubic inch of any pestilential gas in which he lives, not one obscenity or degradation about him ... but shall work its retribution [revenge] though every order of society, up to the proudest of the proud.'

To a Victorian, Dickens's description of Tom's was as scary as a horror film is to us! His story of little Jo, the poor orphan street sweeper in *Bleak House*, is his warning to the public of how the pox would get them. Jo catches the smallpox from the foul, festering air of the slum. He dies from it, but not before infecting the novel's heroine – the lovely Esther – showing that poor and well-to-do alike could catch the pox.

Victorian readers (and modern readers too) wept buckets at the death of Jo and the illness of poor Esther, whose beauty was marked for ever by pockmarks (many of the readers would be horribly pocked too as they sat over the novel with their hankies).

Dickens's writing reached a huge audience through serialization in the papers – and his plotlines were followed as eagerly as Eastenders and Buffy are now. He forced well-off Londoners to imagine (and sympathize with) their less fortunate neighbours and had a big influence in persuading the government that the slums had to be cleaned up.

Though smallpox was feared like the plague at least early doctors figured out how to do something sensible about it – rather than treating it with abracadabra charms and headless chickens, as they did with the plague.

The Cure that Saved the Queen's Skin

Most of the medicines in this book have had more holes in them than a piece of Swiss cheese but one old wives' tale was surprisingly effective. It was thought in Tudor times that hanging pieces of red cloth in the windows would prevent smallpox sufferers being left with nasty scars all over their skin. It was discovered much later by Dr Niels Finsen of Copenhagen that it is the rays of the sun that cause scarring – these can be filtered out with red cloth or paper.

When Queen Elizabeth I (she reigned from 1558 to 1603) caught smallpox her doctor wrapped her from head to toe in red cloth and put her on a red matress. The treatment worked. Liz was left with relatively smooth skin. It was rumoured, however, that the pox left her as bald as an egg – she always wore a wig to cover her shiny pate.

In fact it wasn't a doctor (we're still waiting to hear something good about doctors) but a brave woman who first fought back against smallpox. Lady Mary Wortley Montagu was the wife of the ambassador to the Turkish Sultan. She noticed that in Turkey many people were treated against smallpox. This meant someone, usually an old woman, would make a cut in your skin and put a bit of a smallpox pustule in it .

OK. Say it. Euurgh.

The theory was that the healthy person would get a mild dose of smallpox. (Sometimes they could get a strong dose and die.) If they survived, which they usually did, full-blown, killer smallpox could no longer chop them down. Lady Montagu was very interested because she had survived smallpox – her illness had left her with no eyelashes but lots of scars. Also her adored young brother had died of the illness at the age of twenty.

Lady Montagu came back to London. In London she made a truly terrible decision for any mother. Because no one really knew what the operation meant, she gambled her daughter's life that it would work. In 1721, at the court of King George I and in front of a roomful of top doctors, Lady Montagu's four-year-old daughter was injected with the pus from a smallpox sore. Little Lady Montagu survived and history was changed for ever!

King George himself now got interested. He decided on a royal experiment. Six prisoners at Newgate were promised a royal pardon if they took part in his little test. (History does not record what the prisoners said when told they they had a choice of the pox or the gallows ...) Luckily they too survived – or the King might have got a bad name. The operation spread and even the Prince of Wales's children were jabbed.

But the practice was risky and some people did die. People who had been treated this way could also infect healthy people and start off fresh plagues of smallpox.

A new breakthrough came when a young doctor called Edward Jenner overheard a dairymaid say, 'I shall never have an ugly pockmarked face because I have had cowpox.' Jenner learnt the old wives' tale that people who had cowpox – a disease a bit like

smallpox but much milder which (surprise, surprise) affected cows – never caught the scary speckled monster itself.

Jenner studied cowpox and became convinced that catching it could prevent smallpox. He waited and waited to prove his theory. In May 1796 a milkmaid caught cowpox and Jenner took some of the fluid out of her pustules. He then injected a healthy eight-year-old boy called James Phipps (I hope he asked his parents) with it. Hey presto! Phipps survived – and proved to be safe from smallpox.

Jenner had triumphed. But the more traditional doctors – who were often guilty of being real sticks-in-the-mud – refused to believe him. The President of the Royal Society of Physcians refused to publish Jenner's discovery. But gradually other doctors – including the doctors at London's Smallpox and Innoculation Hospital – believed him and tried his method out.

Gradually his fame spread and soon he was a real celebrity. In America President Thomas Jefferson had eighteen members of his family innoculated. Even Napoleon was a big fan.

When the English asked for some prisoners of war back the tiny Frenchman refused. But when Napoleon heard that Jenner wanted them back he exclaimed, 'Ah, it is Jenner. I cannot refuse Jenner anything.'

Smallpox is the only disease man can claim to have wiped out. In 1980 the World Health Organization (an organization that looks after the world's health) said that smallpox had been wiped out throughout the world. Luckily both America and Russia have kept a jar of smallpox in the fridge to use as a vaccine in case the disease ever comes back. (The American jar is kept in a padlocked fridge, in a bunker which is under constant electronic surveillance.)

CHAPTER EIGHT

The White Death

If I told you that two hundred years ago there was a deadly, disgusting disease that was actually quite trendy among rich and arty Londoners, you'd think I was joking, wouldn't you?

The disease was nicknamed the 'White Death' and killed more people in human history than the plague. Some people think it was the greatest killer in the history of our whole species. But strangely, strong and healthy people pretended to catch this revolting disease in order to be fashionable. And we're not talking about a slimming disease here – one that'll make you look like someone in a magazine who could do with a few square meals!

The White Death was really, really nasty. Here is how you'd feel if you caught it:

First you would get hot flushed cheeks, then you'd begin to feel tired. You'd start coughing. Soon you'd start coughing up a thick, yellowish, snotty phelgm. The phlegm would turn bloody, your bright cheeks would fade and with terrible pain you would simply waste away. (I know fashion hurts sometimes, but give me eyebrow rings [yuck] or platforms any day.)

It's no wonder that the White Death was also called consumption. It consumed its victims like a raging fire. (Its proper medical name is tuberculosis or TB.)

White Death is caused by tiny bacilli that live all around us – in water, grass, mud and hay. A TB-infected lung can hold ten billion bacilli, some of which can be easily spared to come spluttering out when a consumptive coughs all over you. No wonder the white death spread like ... er ... the plague.

In the 1800s seven in ten people in London became infected with the TB bug and at least one of them died.

Many of our ancestors had the bug swimming around in their tummies. But strangely most of them didn't actually catch the disease. Some doctors even believe that the bug was able to do more harm to people who were sad – because their anti-bug fighting systems would be unhappy too and have their guard down.

Unfortunately there were a lot of sad people around in London.

It was always likely to be the poor and those packed like sardines into smelly slums who were in most danger of being consumed by consumption.

This was the time of the Industrial Revolution – which history teachers say made Britain the motor [engine, not car] of the whole world. Smoke stacks and pumping machines appeared everywhere. Peasants were torn away from the land and sent to work in black, grimy factories.

For centuries these peasants – father and son, mother and daughter – had lived in the same old villages, looking after the same couple of cows and sheep (well, the sheep's children and grandchildren). Suddenly patterns of life which had gone on for centuries were torn up like old rubbish.

Sick Londoners appeared everywhere. Pale wraiths coughed their phlegm-spattered way to the grave. In the 1800s one in four deaths were from consumption.

Sick Fashion

Funnily enough (somone must have been laughing), TB became the first fashion victim's disease. Before the 1800s people thought it was beautiful to be stout and strong-looking. But now the consumptive look was actually copied by some people. Why?

A) Because Queen Victoria's beautiful daughter Vicky caught consumption and all the ladies wanted to look like her

B) Because some people believed that you could only catch consumption if you were artistic and spiritual

C) Because if you survived consumption you had a good chance of fighting off other deadly and unfashionable diseases like cholera

D) Consumptives didn't have to fight at Waterloo against the French emperor Napoleon.

Answer B) So many artists and poets creating away in their dark and damp attics caught consumption that some doctors thought you could only get the disease if you were artistic! The consumptive look – thin, pale, deathly – became nuttily fashionable. Some rich ladies even copied the look with whitening powder and potions that included the deadly poison, arsenic. One famous French writer pretended to be consumptive even though he was perfectly healthy. He did this because people wouldn't take him seriously as an artist if he was hale and hearty!

The Pre-Raphaelite painters showed women who looked more like ghosts than flesh and blood, trailing their long hair over weeping streams or drooping like damp washing in their chairs.

The mood was meant to be spiritual and sad. It was certainly very wet.

The great poet John Keats was probably responsible for more wannabe consumptives than any other suffering genius. Keats, the son of a humble stable keeper, was a very romantic poet with long, curling locks of hair and lustrous black eyes (a sort of pop star of his day).

He went around with his fellow Romantics like Shelley, but

some snobs thought he wasn't enough of a toff to be an artist and nicknamed him the 'Cockney Poet'. Keats had trained to be an apothecary – a bit like an early version of a doctor – at St Thomas' hospital before deciding that poetry was more his thing. Sadly his medical training didn't help him when he caught the White Death.

Lots of Keats's poetry was about consumption, such as these famous lines:

Where youth grows pale, and spectre thin, and dies

Where but to think is to be full of sorrow

And leaden-eyed despair.

In fact Keats didn't have long to be miserable. He died from consumption at the age of twenty-six.

Other great writers like Charlotte, Emily and Anne Bronte (the whole family, practically) also died from TB. So did the author of *Treasure Island*, Robert Louis Stevenson. So many writers died, in fact, that it was a wonder there were any occupied attics left!

Doc Consumption?

Consumption wasn't all bad news. It was responsible for something all the doctors in London hadn't been able to do. Was this:

A) Provoking the invention of pain-relieving anaesthetics, because if you take just the right amount of arsenic you can't feel anything, but don't actually die

B) Inspiring more great poetry and art than other disease

C) Because it rid London of leprosy

D) Because the blood that consumptives coughed up was a great cure for typhoid?

ANSWER: C) Leprosy, a disease that produced horrible disfigurements in its victims, had been seen as God's punishment for sin for centuries. Henry II had lepers burnt at the stake without allowing them a funeral. His grandson Edward I was a bit nicer - he allowed lepers funerals, then buried them alive. Leprosy is from the same bug family as TB - and leprosy disappeared at the same time TB attacked London. Scientists think that TB killed off leprosy as a

As usual the doctors didn't have a clue (they're not coming out of this very well, are they?).

Some advised poor consumptives to find a friendly wet nurse and suck on her bosoms (she'd have to be very friendly!). Or they were told to go and sit in a barn and inhale the smell of cows.

In cases where surgeons with their saws and big knives got involved – consumptives' lungs or joints were simply hacked off!

For the rich, consumption started a whole new trend of fancy hotels-cum-hospitals which were called sanatoriums. Londoners would travel to places like the Swiss Alps where pretty nurses would mop their brow and they'd take long steam baths and play tiddlywinks with the other guests.

These sanatoriums were very big on washing and keeping clean and they started the trend of using lino or linoleum on their floor. This plastic floor stuff was much cleaner than carpet or floorboards. The idea was that bugs can hide in the cracks of floorboards or the hair of carpets – but with lino they've got nowhere to run to.

By the end of the 1800s, as London got cleaner and more orderly, TB began to die out. In fact some people believe that

the invention of ordinary things like lino and window panes –
which lets in the light that kills the darkness-loving TB bugs –
had more to do with the way the White Death vanished than
anything the doctors did!

The Bald Bug

In 1882 Robert Koch, a German scientist we've come
across already, discovered that the cause of TB was
a bacterium (what we would call a tiny bug). Under
his lovely microscope it looked just like a seahorse –
without a mane of hair.

In overcrowded and poor parts of London, TB is back. New types
of TB are super scary. They are able to fight all the drugs that
we can throw at them.

CHAPTER NINE

The Spanish Lady

Compared to the other creepy-crawly, yucky-pus-ey, stinky-horrid diseases in this book, flu doesn't sound like much of a plague.

Who hasn't had the flu?

It can be sweaty and feverish but there is something almost cosy about flu. It means a few days off school, bed, hot drinks and lots of mollycoddling. You might think there are worse things in the world.

But if you had visited London in the winter of 1918 you'd change your mind. There was nothing more dreaded than a case of flu.

London in those far-off days was just getting used to the deaths of thousands of young men in the battlefields against the Germans in World War I. These young men had had a terrible time stuck in muddy, foul trenches. But bad as fighting the Germans had been, flu was worse. Here is what the writer Edmund Wilson remembered about being on duty in a hospital during the Great War:

[my fellow worker] was an elderly undertaker, who went around
in felt slippers, with a lantern and a kind of nightcap on his
head. He knew just how to handle dead bodies. We would put
them on a stretcher and carry them down to a basement room
where we sometimes had to pile them up like dogs. They were
buried in big common ditches.

As the young men who had managed to not get shot or blown up came back from war – to wailing mums and dads, sisters, wives and girlfriends – they brought back with them a flu bug which was like no flu bug anybody had ever seen.

People called this flu bug the Spanish Lady as they thought it had come from Spain. As you can imagine, the Spanish didn't like this name very much and called it the Naples Soldier and said it came from Italy. Others called it the Flanders Grippe and blamed the Flemish!

First people noticed a headache, then their eyes started to burn. Shivers would shake them, but no amount of fires and blankets could keep them warm. Then came waking nightmares as the fever kicked in.

Their faces and limbs turned brownish purple and their feet turned black. As death came calling they would gasp for breath. Flu killed by drowning its victim's lungs in reddish liquid.

Londoners (like people from the icebergs of the Antarctic to the Jungles of India) started dying ... and dying ... and they didn't stop.

The newspapers gave lots of advice.

THE NEWS OF THE WORLD

3 November 1918

Wash inside nose with soap and water each night and morning; force yourself to sneeze night and morning, then breathe deeply; do not wear a muffler; take sharp walks regularly and walk home from work; eat plenty of porridge.

Of course a Londoner could wash his nose hairs every morning without fail and still be struck down by flu. (You know that what you read in the newspapers is not always true.)

The flu did what the Great War (World War I) couldn't and almost shut London down. Theatres and churches closed. People stopped going to work. It attacked the humblest and the grandest. King George V got the flu (he recovered, lucky man). The Prime Minister David Lloyd George sweated the fever out in a week when it rained all day every day. In fact it seemed as if everybody had the flu!

The streets were sprayed with chemicals. Some offices and factories changed their no-smoking rules, hoping that tobacco would protect against the flu. In some places it became illegal to cough or spit in public.

Children made up ryhmes about the new plague. One went like this:

I had a little bird

Its name was Enza

I opened the window

And in-flu-enza

Other people only went out wearing funny gauze (a kind of cotton) masks over their noses and mouths. In some places it became illegal not to wear these masks and smart alecks did all sorts of funny things to them. One man had his embroidered with a skull and crossbones. A secretary attached blue wings to her mask.

Everything was tried from medieval remedies like enemas (washing out your bottom with water) to bleeding, castor oil, morphine and cold baths. Some people tied cucumbers to their ankles or put potatoes in their pockets. One mum (who perhaps had been knocking the gin back) buried her daughter kneck-high in onions.

But nothing worked. And then as suddenly as it came, flu vanished.

Flu had killed 228,000 people in England. America suffered even more, losing half a million people. Worldwide it killed maybe fifty million people. Unlike other plagues that went for children and grandparents this bug went for healthy, young adults. In America the life expectancy went down to thiry-eight years.

The hunt for the killer flu bug

We still don't definitely know what caused normal, boring old flu to become a killer plague in 1918. Some people at the time thought the Germans were bombing them with bugs. If they were it didn't work, since plenty of Germans died too. Others thought killer flu was the revenge of wicked war, terrible trenches and mustard gas.

Today there are some people who claim that flu came from Outer Space. (They don't seem to agree whether it flew in from Mars or Venus.)

Scientists more recently have discovered that flu is caused by a virus that looks like a spiky transparant ball with a worm inside.

But why was the 1918 flu so bad?

Nearly eighty years after the terror of the great flu, a group of scientists went on an expedition and dug up the corpse of an Eskimo woman (they called her Lucy) who had died from it. She was frozen solid in the ice of Alaska. By examing the flu bugs that had also frozen inside her, they hope to find out exactly what happened.

The scientists are getting closer to solving the riddle, but they've got no definite answers yet. The best guess so far is that the 1918 flu somehow passed from pigs to humans. (A sick army cook in Kansas, where many people think the whole thing started, may have infected the whole world.)

Could it happen again? We've got super-duper vaccines that can protect us from many types of flu. But if a new deadly killer bug – from pigs or chickens or whatever – mixed with human flu and caught us on the hop ... who knows?

Some people think that a worldwide killer plague could be set off by something as simple as someone with flu sneezing on a bunch of chickens. This could cause human and chicken flu bugs to mix and set up a sinister new strain. So remember next time you go egg-collecting not to sneeze.

This rhyme says it all:

If we but knew

The cause of flu

And whence it comes and what to do

I think that you

And we folks too

Would hardly get in such a stew

Do you?

Some Pestilential Places to Visit

Broadgate, in East London, was the site of several huge plague pits. People excavating the underground and the modern station kept digging up bodies. Despite the history of the Black Death in London no plague pits have been excavated and there is no plague museum. The best place to visit if you're really interested in the Black Death is the Plague Museum in Eyam, Derbyshire.

See where the burning of London all began. The Great Fire of London is commemorated by a statue, designed by Christopher Wren, on Monument Street in the City of London.

The Museum of London, at 150 London Wall, London EC2, has a terrific audiovisual section showing how the fire swept through London. www.museum-london.org.uk

Charles Dickens's house, where he wrote Oliver Twist, has been preserved at the **Dickens House Museum**, 48 Doughty Street, London WC1. It is full of Dickens's personal possesions, as well as providing a faithful reconstruction of how a gentleman of the 1830s lived. www.dickensmuseum.com

The legend of Dick Whittington, four times Lord Mayor of London, who came to seek his fortune in the great city accompanied by his trusty cat is remembered by the Whittington Stone on Highgate Hill, London, N19. Nearby is the Whittington – one of London's largest hospitals – which is named after London's most famous mayor.

The beautiful Hampstead house where **John Keats** lived from 1818 to 1820 is now a museum at 10 Keats Grove, London NW3. He wrote 'Ode To A Nightingale' under a plum tree in the garden. www.keatshouse.org.uk

The Old Operating Theatre, Museum and Herb Garret at 9a St Thomas's Street, London SE1, is a fascinating reconstruction of an old surgery. It also features displays of herbs and apothecaries' tools and regular talks and special events. www.thegarret.org.uk

Chelsea Physic Garden, 66 Royal Hospital Road, London SW3, was founded in 1673 by the Society of Apothecaries to study the plants used in medicine. It features medicinal plants as well as rare plants. www.chelseaphysicgarden.co.uk

The Foundling Museum, remembering the work of Captain Thomas Coram, is being refurbished and will be opening in 2004, at 40 Brunswick Square, London WC1. www.coram.org.uk

Alexander Fleming Laboratory Museum, St Mary's Hospital, Praed Street, London W2, is a reconstruction of the lab where Fleming discovered penicillin in 1928. www.medicalmuseums.org

Museum of the Royal College of Surgeons, 35-43 Lincoln's Inn Fields, London WC2, has a large collection of surgical instruments from 1700 to 1900 and skeletons, including that of the famous criminal Jonathan Wild and the 'Irish Giant' Charles Byrne. www.rcseng.ac.uk

Great Ormond Street Hospital, 55 Great Ormond Street, London WC1, has a museum within the famous hospital. But admittance is by apointment only – so please contact the museum in advance. www.medicalmuseums.org

Museum of the Order of St John, St John's Gate, St John's Lane, London EC1, has a Norman crypt and a Tudor Gate house. It records the history of London's first ambulance service. www.medicalmuseums.org

British Red Cross Museum, 9 Grosvenor Square, London SW1, has a collection showing how the British Red Cross carried out its work in war and peace from 1870 to today. They have a fine collection of equipment and badges. www.medicalmuseums.org

Florence Nightingale Museum, St Thomas' Hospital, 2 Lambeth Palace Road, London SE1, features a reconstruction of a ward like the one that the pioneer nurse used in Crimea. www.florence-nightingale.co.uk

The Science Museum, Exhibition Road, South Kensington, London SW7 is one of the biggest and most imaginative science museums in Europe. www.sciencemuseum.org.uk

WATLING ST

If you enjoyed this book, why not try others in the series:

CRYPTS, CAVES AND TUNNELS OF LONDON
by Ian Marchant
Peel away the layers under your feet and discover
the unseen treasures of London beneath the streets.
ISBN 1-904153-04-6

GRAVE-ROBBERS, CUT-THROATS AND POISONERS
OF LONDON
by Helen Smith
Dive into London's criminal past and meet some of its
thieves, murderers and villains.
ISBN 1-904153-00-3

DUNGEONS, GALLOWS AND SEVERED HEADS OF LONDON
by Travis Elborough
For spine-chilling tortures and blood-curdling punishments,
not to mention the most revolting dungeons and prisons you can
imagine.
ISBN 1-904153-03-8

GHOSTS, GHOULS AND PHANTOMS OF LONDON
by Travis Elborough
Meet some of the victims of London's bloodthirsty monarchs,
murderers, plagues, fires and famines - who've chosen to stick
around!
ISBN 1-904153-02-X

RATS, BATS, FROGS AND BOGS OF LONDON
by Chris McLaren
Find out where you can find some of the amazing species
London has to offer the budding naturalist.
ISBN 1-904153-05-4

In case you have difficulty finding any Watling St books in your local bookshop, you can place orders directly through

BOOKPOST
Freepost
PO Box 29
Douglas
Isle of Man
IM99 1BQ

Telephone: 01624 836000
e-mail: bookshop@enterprise.net